DATES IN THE STATES

A COUPLE TRAVELING THE UNITED STATES ON A BUDGET

I0541624

HAUNTED

Mystery Date

Irondequoit, NY

By Dates in the States

"Our passion is travel, and we want to share our adventures to inspire others to explore the world with their loved ones. Dare to live beyond the box."

Dates in the States

INTRODUCTION

Hey there, fellow travelers! We're Crystal & Shane from Dates in the States, and we can't wait to take you on a ghostly adventure you'll never forget! Our blog is all about uncovering the best local events, dishing on delicious eats, hitting invigorating hikes, and discovering quirky roadside attractions. And now, we're adding a dash of the paranormal to the mix!

Welcome to our haunted mystery date book, where we'll whisk you away to the shores of Lake Ontario, to the charming yet eerie Seabreeze neighborhood in Irondequoit, NY. Known for its scenic views, the heart-pounding rides of its historic amusement park, and the soothing hum of the waves, Seabreeze has a secret side that's just dying to be explored. Beneath its picturesque facade lies a tangled web of secrets, whispers, and unsolved mysteries that have haunted the town for generations.

White Lady's Castle

Lake Shore Blvd
Rochester, NY 14617

Start your visit with a walk through Durand Eastman Park while it's still light out. You may take any trail you'd like, but make sure White Lady's Castle is where you start or end.

Located along Lakeshore Boulevard in Rochester, NY, White Lady's Castle is actually the remnants of a stone structure from the early 20th century, possibly a dining hall or picnic shelter. Its mysterious appearance has sparked local legends, including the tale of the White Lady.

A short drive from Seabreeze, you can park in the lot across the street and take a brief walk to the ruins. The stairs lead to scenic views of Lake Ontario, and the combination of ruins, lake views, and surrounding woods creates a memorable and slightly eerie atmosphere, perfect for those interested in the legend or simply enjoying the scenery.

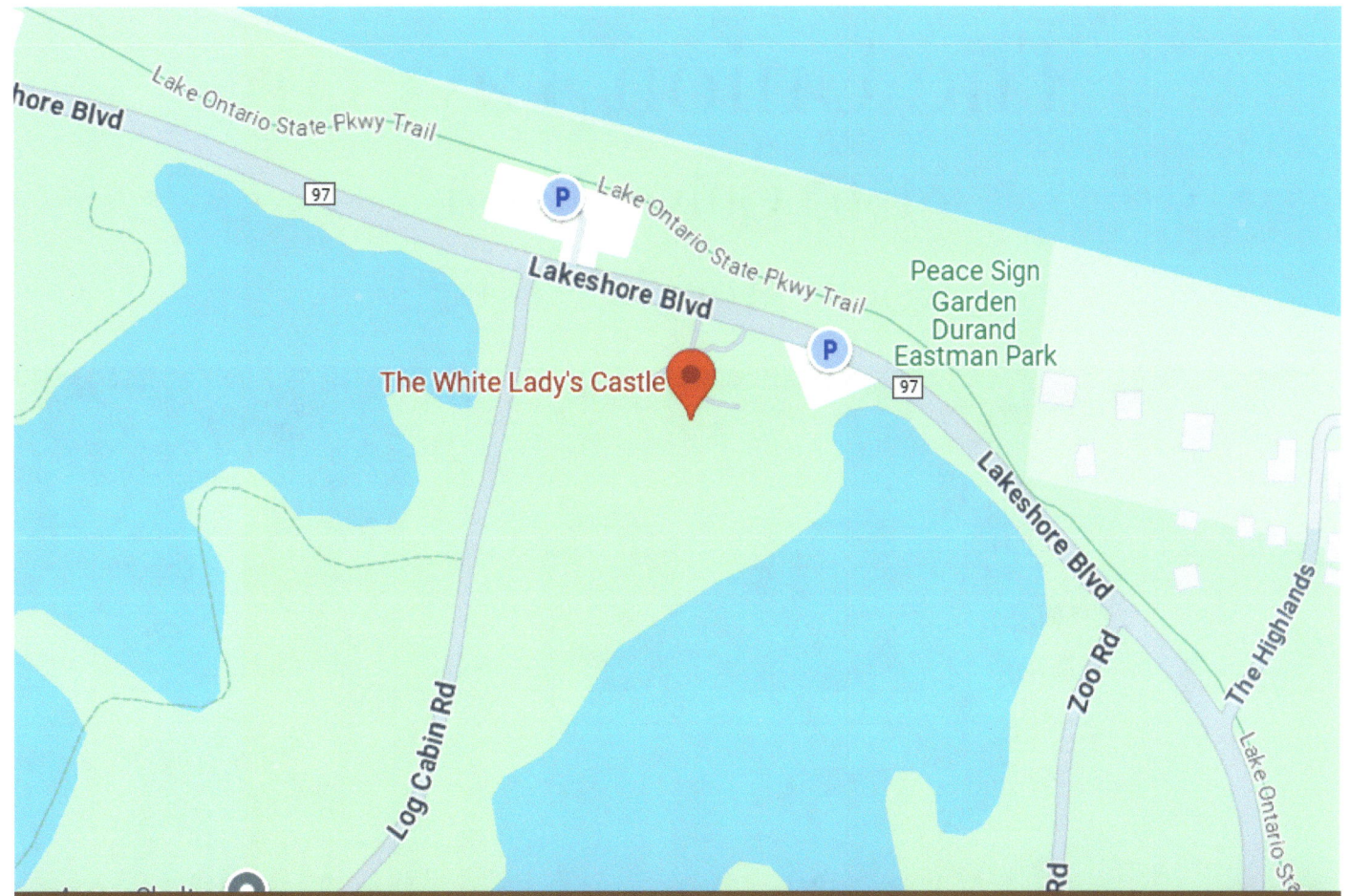

The legend of the White Lady is one of the most famous ghost stories in the Rochester area. According to the tale, the White Lady was a woman who lived in a large mansion near the current site of the ruins. She was reportedly searching for her missing daughter, who had either run away or been murdered. The grieving mother, wearing a flowing white nightgown, would roam the area with her two dogs, looking for her lost child.

Some versions of the story suggest that the woman drowned in Lake Ontario while searching for her daughter, while others say she met a more violent end. Regardless of the version, it's said that her restless spirit still wanders the park, and sightings of the White Lady and her dogs have been reported by visitors.

Durand Eastman Park is part of the greater Rochester park system and offers beautiful views of Lake Ontario, walking trails, and picnic areas. The area around White Lady's Castle is particularly popular with locals and visitors who are drawn not only by its natural beauty but also by the eerie atmosphere that the legend brings to the site.

The Union Tavern

4565 Culver Road,
Rochester, NY 14622

The Union Tavern, with its rich and eerie history, has stories that stretch back to the 1800s. The original owner was a pirate seeking refuge in the quiet neighborhood of Seabreeze. His name was Mr. Woodman, and he and his wife lived out their days in what was then known as the Woodman House. After their passing, the street they lived on was named Woodman Road, which we now know as Culver Road.

The tavern's next owner, Mr. Bradstreet, met a tragic end when he was trampled by his own horses right in front of the Union Tavern. Today, it's said that Mr. Bradstreet's restless spirit haunts the cupola at the top of the tavern. If you ever catch a glimpse of a shadowy figure amidst the neon lights up there, you just might be seeing him.

Both the Woodman and Bradstreet families were buried nearby, under what is now the parking lot of Big Al's Eatery. In the 1800s, there was no embalming or preservation, just simple wooden boxes. While it's known their bodies were laid to rest there, no trace of their remains can be found today. The Union Tavern, with its storied past and ghostly presence, continues to be a place where history and the supernatural linger together.

Before reopening the establishment as we know it today, the new owners were keenly aware of the tavern's haunted reputation. They even had their realtor, one of our neighbors, hire a paranormal investigator to check out the premises. What they found remains a mystery, but it's clear that the Union Tavern's past continues to cast a shadow over its present.

SO, now that you know a little spooky history about the tavern - this is your second stop for your haunted mystery date!

Stop in, grab a drink and sit at the bar and ask the bartender if there are any ghost stories they can share!

3RD STOP

Shamrock Jack's Irish Pub

4554 Culver Road,
Rochester, NY 14622

Now that you've grabbed a drink at Union Tavern and hopefully heard some ghost stories, it's time to get a bite to eat at Shamrock Jack's Irish Pub across the street.

Back in the 1800s, Shamrock Jack's was a private residence owned by a man named Dobson. Dobson, an older gentleman with a serious gambling habit, made the fatal mistake of getting involved with the mob. When he couldn't repay his debts, the mob came to collect—permanently. They killed Dobson right in the basement of what is now Shamrock Jack's. To this day, employees are a bit squeamish about heading down there, especially since some have reported feeling an eerie presence or having wine and beer bottles mysteriously thrown at their heads, which they attribute to Dobson's restless spirit.

Dobson isn't the only ghost at Shamrock Jack's. A little girl, believed to have died at Seabreeze Amusement Park, is known to visit the pub when the park is closed. She's often spotted on the first floor, playfully switching TV channels and flickering the lights.

Shamrock Jack's also has a colorful history from the days of Prohibition. The savvy owners of the time built hidden doorways disguised as bookshelves and other everyday objects to conceal their illegal stash of alcohol. Some of the staff may show you where these hidden doorways are if you ask!

With Lake Ontario just down the street, they had a convenient route for importing booze from Canada, making Shamrock Jack's a popular spot for locals looking to enjoy a forbidden drink. Even the Fire Department got in on the action, operating as a speakeasy and importing their own Canadian spirits, all without arousing suspicion.

As you leave Shamrock Jack's, look across the street, and you may notice a small cobblestone building. This unassuming structure, now in the middle of a parking lot, was once part of an estate owned by an old man who loved his evening drinks with friends. To escape the house, he built a man cave in his backyard, which is the cobblestone building you see today. Look closely, and you might spot the outline of glass bottles set into the stone on either side of the door—a silent nod to its past as a gathering place for those seeking a good time away from prying eyes.

FINAL STOP
Seabreeze Amusement Park
4600 Culver Road,
Rochester, NY 14622

Next stop on your haunted mystery date is Seabreeze Amusement Park, a place of joy and thrills...and a few lingering spirits. If you're visiting when the park is open, and time allows, don't miss the chance to go in and experience its historic rides and atmosphere. But if you find yourself there in the off-season, take a stroll around the park's outer perimeter. Peering through the fences, especially in the dark, offers a view that's equal parts eerie and nostalgic.

The area is safe for walking after dinner, making it the perfect spot for a nighttime stroll together. Wander down past Marge's, out to the lighthouse, and back—just the two of you and the whispers of the past.

Locals might claim that no one has ever been killed at Seabreeze Amusement Park, but the truth is far more unsettling. Two tragic incidents involving young girls have been recounted over the years, although there may be more that remain hidden in the park's shadowy past. One girl met her end on the Jack Rabbit, one of the oldest roller coasters in the country. Standing up just before entering the tunnel, she was tragically decapitated. Another girl was fatally injured on the Haunted House ride, a once-popular attraction that is no longer in operation. She stepped off the ride halfway through to scare her friend, but her foot got caught in the track. Unable to free herself in time, her leg was run over, and she bled out before reaching the hospital.

These unfortunate souls are believed to be among the spirits that still linger at Seabreeze Amusement Park. Their presence can sometimes be sensed in the creaking of the rides, glimpsed as fleeting shadows across the grounds, or felt as a sudden chill in the air. One of these restless spirits is said to be the ghost of a little girl who, during the summer, roams the park alongside other ghosts drawn to its lively energy. When the park is closed for the season, she makes her way over to Shamrock Jack's Irish Pub, where she's known to playfully switch TV channels and flicker the lights on the first floor.

Add Your Photos

Keepsakes

Thank you for joining us on this mystery date adventure! We hope you've enjoyed the delightful experiences and memorable moments we've crafted just for you in Irondequoit, NY.

But the adventure doesn't stop here! Keep exploring exciting mystery dates in other cities and uncover new romantic experiences across the U.S. by visiting our website, DatesInTheStates.com. There, you can purchase both physical copies and digital downloads of our mystery date books. Plus, don't miss out on our Mystery Date Book Club, where you can receive a brand-new mystery date book every month!

Tag us in your date photos on social media! @datesinthestates

About the Creators

Crystal, the writer and creator, is a storyteller at heart. When she's not uncovering hidden gems for the next date night idea, she runs her own digital marketing company, helping small businesses improve their content marketing, increase visibility in their communities, and streamline their online presence.
Visit: crystalstatskey.com

Shane, her husband and partner in adventure, is a dedicated personal trainer and the owner of Beekstar Fitness in Irondequoit, NY. He specializes in working with clients who have limited mobility, helping them build muscle and focus on pain areas so they can regain strength and confidence in their daily lives.
Visit: beekstarfitness.com

Crystal and Shane have explored every U.S. state except Alaska (coming soon!) and are now visiting countries in alphabetical order. Whether road-tripping or curating Mystery Date experiences, they're always chasing their next adventure.

Want to be featured?

MYSTERY DATE BOOK PACKAGES

—

Are you a small business looking to reach new customers? Feature your business in our next Mystery Date Book! Choose from our partnership packages below to connect with couples seeking unique experiences and exclusive deals.

Package One

LOCAL LOVE LISTING

—

A quick shoutout to show you're part of the neighborhood vibe.

Listed in the "Local Love" section of your designated neighborhood date book

Includes business name, address, and social link

Optional: Offer a small promo (e.g., 10% off for book holders)

1 social media shout-out when the book launches

$45

Package Two

FEATURE STOP

—

You're not just a business— you're part of the experience.

Marked as a "Must-Stop" on a Mystery Date

Full-page feature in the book with your story, offerings and photo

Includes 1 social media feature — a dedicated post and story highlighting your business

Note: To ensure each feature is genuine and experience-based, we require a hosted visit prior to inclusion.

$95

Package Three

PARTNER & SELLER

—

Be the spot and the source.

Everything in Tier 2

PLUS: Option to sell the Mystery Date Books at your location

Includes a bulk purchase of 10 books (yours to price + sell)

Keep 100% of the profits from in-store sales

Bonus: Tag as an official pickup location in our promotions

$150

Prices are subject to change

Feel free to reach us at any time by sending us an email to say hi and to learn more! We look forward to hearing from you.

| www.datesinthestates.com | datesinthestatesblog@gmail.com |

Sponsors & Affiliates

Our sponsors and affiliates help make our adventures possible! Explore the amazing brands and businesses that support our community.

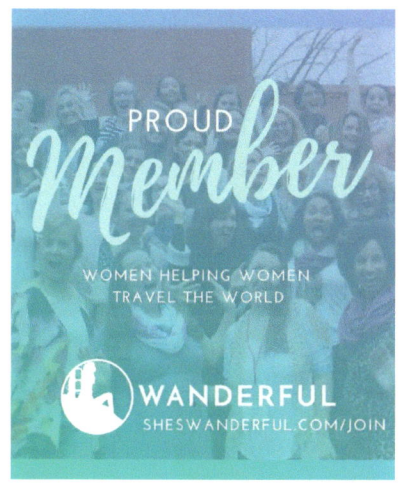  

Wanderful

Wanderful is a global community for women who love to travel. Connect, explore, and join a local hub near you!

Join our Book Club!

Join our Mystery Date Book Club and be part of a travel-inspired community, discovering unique local adventures together!

HomeExchange

HomeExchange lets you swap homes with travelers worldwide for authentic, affordable stays. Join today and travel differently!

Shop our books at a store near you!

Little Button Craft
658 South Ave.
Rochester, NY 14620

The Pawsitive Cat Cafe
120 East Ave. Ste 100
Rochester, NY 14604

Yesterday's Muse Books
32 West Main St.
Webster, NY 14580

Writers & Books
740 University Ave,
Rochester, NY 14607

Littleberger Florist
63 North Avenue,
Webster, NY 14580

Flight Wine Bar
262 Exchange Blvd,
Rochester, NY 14608

Scents by Design
728 University Ave,
Rochester, NY 14607

Union Tavern
4565 Culver Rd,
Irondequoit, NY 14622

DATES IN THE STATES

A COUPLE TRAVELING THE UNITED
STATES ON A BUDGET

Contact Us

🌐

datesinthestates.com

✉️

datesinthestatesblog@gmail.com

📍

Based in Rochester, NY

CONNECT WITH US ON SOCIAL!

@DATESINTHESTATES

_____